First published in Great Britain in 2006 by Comma Press
3rd Floor, 24 Lever Street, Manchester M1 1DW
www.commapress.co.uk

The lyrics to 'It's a Fine Day' are reprinted by kind permission of Complete Music.

A CIP catalogue record of this book is available from the British Library

ISBN: 1-905583-06-0
EAN: 978-1- 905583-06-5

The publishers gratefully acknowledge assistance from the Arts Council England
North West, as well as the support of Literature Northwest:
www.literaturenorthwest.co.uk

Set in Bembo by XL Publishing Services, Tiverton
Printed and bound in England by SRP Ltd, Exeter.

bad leg

EDWARD BARTON

For Pete, -2002

CONTENTS

Bad Leg

The handbill read,
'Do you suffer from Bad Leg?
Send off today for our Bad Leg Pills.'
I do, and I will:
I don't want Bad Leg.

The Bill Man said,
'I suffered from Bad Leg.
I sent away for some Bad Leg Pills,
and now I'm not ill:
no more Bad Leg.'

'O Bill Man,' I said,
'I suffer from Bad Leg:
we were out looking for eggs when my friend saw a hornbill
high over that hill,
and I got Bad Leg.

My friend sped ahead;
I lagged behind with Bad Leg.
I thought it was a little bit of Leg Hurt until
I lost all leg skills:
I've got Bad Leg.'

The Bill Man said,
'Sell your bed! Buy some segs!
Sort your legs out with our Bad Leg Pills:
get back your leg skills.
Why have Bad Leg?'

I'll sell my bed,
take my coat down from the peg:
I'll sort my legs out with your Bad Leg Pills,
and run up that hill.
Goodbye to Bad Leg!

Big Arsed Girl

I'd eaten dinner,
done the dishes –
keeping my hands warm
in the washing-up water –
knock on the door.
Huh?
It was a big arsed girl.
It was a big arsed girl
in a reddish dress.
She had nothing on
but that dress –
some shoes.
She said,
'Lift up your vest,
and show me your shopping.'

Biting and Chewing

They're biting and chewing.
They're nesting and screwing.
They're laying and hatching.
I'm itching and scratching.

The Bobble on her Bobble Hat

The sky was like a dirty pond.
The clouds were old grey bread.
The bobble on her bobble-hat
was bigger than her head.

I walked halfway across the road
and looked at her and said,
'My Grandad's got a giant cake;
it's locked up in our shed.'

She walked halfway across the road
and looked at me and said,
'My Grandma keeps her gentlemen
upstairs beneath her bed.'

We stood halfway across the road.
I looked at her and said,
'The bobble on your bobble hat
is bigger than your head.'

The bobble on her bobble-hat
bob-bobbled as she said,
'I think it's time we left the road
And looked inside that shed.'

The sky was like a dirty pond.
The clouds were grey old bread.
The bobble on her bobble-hat
was bigger than her head.

Cathedral Marmalade

My Grandma made Cathedral Marmalade.
She held the evening sky
of every summer that tried
its best to pass her by
in the stained glass glow of those tall jars.

My Grandma made Cathedral Marmalade.
The well-blessed congregation
prayed and praised their nation,
host and lowly station,
and dreamt of rows of gold-smeared toast.

Dad and the Doodlebug

In nineteen forty-four
when my dad was fifteen
he was the biggest kid
in the school canteen.
He was bigger than the teachers
and the biggest dinner lady –
when he went out in the playground
the playground went shady.

The Nazis had a bomb
we called the Doodlebug –
it flew over the Channel
with a 'chug, chug, chug.'
As soon as you heard it,
you had to love that sound,
'cos when the chugging stopped,
the bugger dropped down.

Now out of all London
most of those engines
cut out right over
Croydon and Penge.
And as Dad lived in Penge,
and went to school in Croydon,
when it came to Doodlebugs,
he couldn't avoid 'em.

He was walking past
the old Albert pub
when it got a direct hit
from a Wobblegrub.
My dad was picked up
on a wave of heat
and thrown right across
Harrington Street.

He sat on the pavement,
feeling fairly queer –
that bomb had jumbled breakfast;
eels and pigs ear.
He was staring at the sky,
tongue counting his teeth,
when he felt a little lump
underneath his beef.

He was thinking he'd get up
when he heard a warden shout,
'Move this massive schoolboy,
there's a hand sticking out!'
It took a dozen volunteers
to haul him vertical.
One passed him up his cap –
he wasn't hurt at all.

Unlike the little chap
that Dad had landed on –
whatever a burton is,
he'd gone for one.
Dad undid his blazer
and covered up the man.
He walked home in his shirt –
the man went in a van.

My Dad's big regret
was that the war was won
while he was still too young
to run round with a gun.
He'd tried to enlist
but was easily caught –
they were fooled by his size,
but not by his shorts.

When the Yanks crossed the Rhine
there was no-one as bitter
as my Dad. (Well, perhaps,
I suppose, Adolf Hitler.)
So don't ask my Dad
what he did in the war –
the poor old feller's
on a minus score.

Digging a Hole

'Why are you digging a hole?'
'I don't have a magic wand.'
'What sort of hole is it?'
'It's a fish pond.'
'Why is the hole so deep?'
'The fish are very tall.'
'Why are you doing all this?'
'It's what the fish wish.'
'What have you put the hole
in front of the front step for?'
'So the fish can get in and out of the house.'
'How?' 'Each fish gets a drawer
with a key in it for the front door.'

'I know what you're doing.
I know you're digging a grave.
My Mum said that neither you
nor your dog know how to behave.
My Grandad said it's a shame
you're not both about to rot.
Can I look at your dog?'
'No, you can't.' 'Why not?'
'You can't see my wife when she's naked
or my sweet dog dead.'
'You're off your bloody nut,
and your wife's long since fled.
That's what my Mum said.'

Dog'll Do

I'm just dawdling around
waiting for the dog.
Where the dog goes,
so do I.
I had just enough love
ready for a dog.
When the dog goes,
so will I.

      Dog'll do, dog'll do.

He can't lift a leg
to leak like a dog.
Where's the wag gone
from his eyes?
He leans on my leg
to suck up breath,
and each breath out
is a sigh.

      Dog'll do, dog'll do.

Fairy Cakes and Angel Cakes

You were so certain that it was Fairy Cakes
that come equipped with feathers of white icing.
Whereas I swore that it was Angel Cakes
that float beneath a pair of nice white wings.

I took a stroll along to Greggs the Bakers
and told the girl there of my fancy
for an Angel and a Fairy Cake.
She sighed, 'We've only got what you can see.'

I asked that sullen girl in Greggs the Bakers;
'Please explain to me the difference
between an Angel and a Fairy Cake.'
She sighed, 'A little over fifty pence.'

So there I was, uncertain in the bakers,
looking like a beggar after handouts,
when a tubby chap nearby cried, 'Cakes!
A subject I can tell a man about.'

This chatty gastronome in Greggs the Bakers
knew our cake with wings was neither my
square Angel nor your simple Fairy Cake,
but yet another named the Butterfly.

Fat Man

Look at the fat man
eating his tea
from a big pan,
flat on one knee;
look at his fat hand
feeding him peas,
potatoes and spam.
He doesn't see me.
In his deep shade I fade
as the red sun smoulders
on the dimpled boulders
of his head and shoulders.

O! Such a show:
he's eating chips.
A pearl of slow
grease drips from his lips
onto that torso
and lazily slips,
to tremble and glow
on the brink of a hip.
He lifts his cup, up and up,
to quaff more beer:
far off, down here,
I shout out, 'cheers!'

That's the last of the jam,
and there's nothing to sup:
his careless hands
relinquish his cup.
All that I am
could fit in that cup.
Hands on his hams,
and he's standing up.
Suppose I fell into the well
of his hot, dark, long,
strong-smelling belly-button,
soft at the bottom.

I once met a man
who saw him sneeze.
He said the fat man
started to wheeze
like a broken brass band,
to bob and to heave;
his innards began
to struggle and seethe,
boiling within his tight skin:
the sneeze hurled the man
until he was slammed
back into a tram.

He blinks and blows,
standing at last:
I stand below
the best-ever arse.
If he took me in tow,
I'd live on grass
to buy him gâteaux,
pâté de fois gras
and figs. I'm a twig in a wig.
All of the worth
of this poor earth
is in his girth.

My tears flow;
my face is slime:
If only he'd slowly
incline his spine,
and let me know
that he wouldn't mind
if I held a toe;
that would leave nine.
'You have so much: may I touch
your smallest toe,
not all of a row?
That done, I'd go.'

Firing Squad

All the girls I gave my all
have formed a firing squad
and look – there's me against that wall,
mouth open like a cod.
Most aim at my heart, O God,
a few straight at my balls!
Sweet Sue packs custard pies and trifles,
the rest mere Enfield rifles.

I've watched the weather work each brick
of that slow falling wall.
Against it I struck matches, scratched itches
and grew so nearly tall.
It's been my blackboard, pub, urinal
and both ends of the pitch;
and every time I kissed Miss Hicks
it chalked her arse a wicket.

Once their satiated figures
swanked round in this silk gown –
so sweethearts, where's my last cigar?
I feel a little down.
The front row grind knees. All frown.
Rings glitter with the triggers.
My wife commands this silent choir.
She'll drop an arm – they'll fire.

It's not because I'm lightly dressed,
I sport a goose's pimples.
Nor is it that I'm so distressed.
The reason is too simple –
they're beautiful. (No blindfold, Jill,
that's overdressing.) Rest
your angry bullets in my breast.
I loved you all the best.

Florescence

I traipse around the woods all day
so not to pause upon her ways,
the way her fingers lift her hair,
the fair, the grey, and hold it there,
and slowly let it fall the way
the wind is with the willow's leaves.

She shuts her eyes against her stare,
she sighs as softly as she breathes.

This is the whitest birch I know–
full moon it shines, no moon it glows
searched out by every stars' small light –
tonight the snow's not quite as white.
Close to, the scars and stretch-marks show,
and so I kiss those distant seams.

I bump around the woods all night.
She smoothes in white and glowing creams.

Garden with a Rabbit and a Ladder

Here's a garden with a rabbit
and a ladder in it.
Half this garden is in shadow,
half in bright sunlight.
The rabbit is almost all white,
and mostly in the light.
The fur around the rabbit's nose
is dark and in the shadow.

Laid beside the rabbit is the
longish wooden ladder.
Half this ladder is in shadow,
half in bright sunlight.
So let's try and get this right
before it turns to night.
No, hang on a mo – I know,
let's just take a photo.

Good at Football

My foot is no good.
I hate my foot.
I throw myself on the concrete.
Tears fall out of my face.

I want to score a goal.
I am no good at football.

I run. I kick. I run.
I fall off my legs.
All my life, not one goal.
I look at the ground.

I want to score a goal.
I am no good at football.

Goalkeeper, look at that big bird in the sky!

GOAL!

I have scored a goal:
I am good at football.

Call me Hero,
Call me Good At Football.
Call me Goal–Scorer.
Queen, you may kiss me.
Give me the golden cup
in the big bath.
Let me bathe in the suds of glory.

I have scored a goal:
I am good at football.

Goodbye and Hello

When we two meet
he says 'Goodbye',
and so do I,
and when he goes
we say 'Hello'.

I run outside
and there he stands
waving a hand.
He says 'Goodbye',
and so do I.

We joke and play.
He makes up games,
no two the same,
then says 'Hello',
not 'Cheerio'.

Today I heard
his voice outside.
'Goodbye', it cried.
The sun was bright,
I said 'Goodnight.'

His grin grew huge.
He donned his hat.
I smiled at that
and rang the bell.
He said, 'Well, well.'

Grandad

Look at my face!
My bones are a jumble thrown on a bed.
Fools with my blood! You bring me fruit –
I want women! Bring me women!
Don't say you have no women:
I can smell them on you –
sweetness, faint against the sweat of fools.

They do not have to talk. They can say nothing.
They do not have to stir the ancient lashes of my old eyes
with the soft breath of a few low words of comfort.
They can just stand at the foot of the bed
by the chart that says, 'Nearly dead',
and eat the fruit.

I want women! Bring me women!
Where are your women? What did you travel here for?
Just to hear me offer commiserations on your imminent loss?
Did you fear I would jump on your private women?
All I can move are my eyes.
Once I bought you all tiny chairs, and I carried them home on
the bus.
Are you blind, insensitive, selfish, cruel, deaf?
If I could raise an arm, I would beat you.

Where are your women? Women in their women's clothes.
Women's shoes done up with women's laces.
Women's wonderful eyes in women's wonderful faces.
Are the women cooking? Kick them out of bed!
Stop looking at the ceiling. Come on now, lads – it's me,
Grandad!
You have made a mistake. You know you should have brought
some women.

Take the money. Sponge your suits. Shine your spades.
This is a useless send-off. I want a woman in each eye.
I want to say goodbye. Don't you know what a woman is for?
You bring me fruit – bring me women! One that can sing.
I will live a little longer while you look around.
I want women! Don't say you have no women:
I can smell them on you –
sweetness, faint against the sweat of fools.

Are they stood behind you?
Are the women stood behind you?
Come out, short women!

Hat On, Hat Off

Picture number one is of my dad:
nice specs, nice tache, nice belly.
Here he's doing something he does well:
he's watching telly.

Picture two shows Dad with brother Pin:
Dad and him aren't friends anymore.
He's just told Pin the final score:
he's seen it before.

When Dad refused to say sorry,
Pin got crosser and crosser.
Look what happened after he told Dad he was a
stupid old tosser.

In picture four, Dad's still hurting Pin,
but he's seen I'm taking pictures,
so he's pulling silly faces and snickering,
'I know what'll fix yer!'

Here's the happy couple once again,
but with something pretty hard to understand:
how did skinny Pin get the upper hand
on the big boss man?

Picture six explains picture five:
Dad's ankle was being tied in knots.
Brother Tim, running round in his bare bot,
was just out of shot.

It's over and done by picture seven:
violence has cleared the air.
Dad's a pear with a stare, Tim's no longer there,
and just look at Pin's hair.

Hit a Man

I want to hit a man,
once, while I still can.
He's got to go down,
and stay on the ground.
I need to see his nose
bleeding on his clothes.
I've not hit anyone.
I wish I had done.

I've given it some thought.
I'm going to walk
along the high street,
and when I meet
some fit young man
I'll stop him, and stand
upon his two feet,
and make the boy bleat.

If he's with his sweetheart,
I'll call her a tart.
When he gets stroppy
and tries to drop me,
I'll drop him, and walk
away from these thoughts,
straight back to this house,
and live like a mouse.

I Lie and I Wonder

I lie and I wonder but I don't really know
how she got all her clothes off in one blinking go.
She'd laugh, 'hop on top', laughing 'faster, go faster;
we'll do all the foreplay straight after'.

I Took off my 'Pants

I took off my 'pants and she said, 'Your cock stinks'.
I said, 'I'm so sorry', and went brightly pink.
She winked as she said, 'Oh, don't worry, it's nice;
it'll help me to find it at night.'

It's a Fine Day

It's a fine day.
People open windows.
They leave their houses,
just for a short while.
They walk by the grass,
and they look at the grass.
They look at the sky.
It's going to be a fine night tonight.
It's going to be a fine day tomorrow.
We will have salad.

I've Got No Chicken But I've Got Five Wooden Chairs

I've got no chicken,
but I've got five wooden chairs.

Chicken just arrived one day,
and, just as easy,
my chicken flew away.

I've got no chicken,
but I've got five wooden chairs.

I placed them in a straight row,
and I lay along them.
Chicken sat on my belly.
I touched the first chair
with my big toe –
O, the roughness of wood –
and, with my longest finger,
the last chair.

I've got no chicken –
had a chicken –
but I've got five wooden chairs.

O, my chicken's gone.
O, my chicken.
My chicken's gone,
my chicken:
and I'm digging a hole,
digging a hole,
digging a hole
for my five wooden chairs.

Knobgob

My name is Knobgob.
All I am for is my Knob and my Gob:
where I can put my Knob,
and what I can put in my Gob.
My name is Knobgob.
Luck has been willing:
Gob full, and Knob filling.
My name is Knobgob.
Born Knob stuck stiff, Gob agog,
I soon found a log:
a branch for my Gob,
a knot-hole for my Knob.

My name is Knobgob.
Luck has been willing;
of fat Gob full and Knob filling
I sing.
But of late, more and more,
a lack sends me to the floor:
my Knob it aches and throbs,
my Gob it sighs and sobs,
for I cannot get,
I cannot get
my Knob in my Gob.

My name is Knobgob.
Soon I will be dead,
for I have greatly bled.
So as not to choke on empty songs,
because my back is long,
I bent my back until it broke:
my Knob is in my Gob.
Wreathe me and grieve for me,
sink me or sack me,

burn me or worm me,
let me rot, or not,
but do not,
do not unstop
my Knob from my Gob.

Ladies

I like the ladies.
I really like the ladies.
When I see the ladies,
I say, 'Hi, ladies',
and the ladies say 'Hi' to me.

When I see that the ladies
are too far away
for me to say, 'Hi ladies',
I wave to the ladies,
and the ladies wave to me.

I like the ladies.
I really like the ladies.
When I see the ladies,
I say, 'Hi, Ladies',
and the ladies say 'Hi' to me.

When I was a baby,
my hair was curly-wavy.
All the girls and ladies
always used to say,
'See! His hair's so curly-wavy.'

I like the ladies.
I really like the ladies.
When I see the ladies,
I say, 'Hi, ladies',
and the ladies say 'Hi' to me.

My mother said to me,
'Be a David not a Davie:
wear a suit of navy,
shave, and act bravely
and gaily with the ladies.'

I like the ladies.
I really like the ladies.
When I see the ladies,
I say, 'Hi, ladies',
and the ladies say 'Hi' to me.

Love or Dirt?

I met a woman by my house.
I asked would she like to come in my house.
She asked, 'Is it clean?'
'It is full of dirt,' I replied.
The woman went away.

I met a Love and Dirt expert.
The Love and Dirt expert explained,
'The woman wants a clean house.
This house is full of dirt.
My advice: get rid of the dirt.
The house will be clean.
The woman will return.'

I put the dirt
in piles of different sorts of dirt.
The Love and Dirt expert returned.
'No, no, no, no, no, no.
That is tidy, but not clean.
You must choose:
love or dirt.
Love or dirt.
Dirt or love.'
'Can I clean the dirt?'
'You cannot clean the dirt.
You must choose:
love or dirt.
Love or dirt.
Dirt or love.'

Dirt has everything in it.
Dirt is history.
History is dirt.
Dirt has everything in it,
but all the people say
love is the greatest thing.
I do not recognise my house
She could eat from my spoons,
wash up in my sink;
she could bathe in my bath.
This cleanliness hurts my eyes.
Beasts and insects went away.
Soap in a dish by the bath.
I must choose:
love or dirt?
Love or dirt?
Dirt or love?

I stand with my broom by my house.
The Love and Dirt expert says, 'Excellent.'
My eyeballs glow.
I will wait for the woman.
I will ask if she would like to come in my house.
She will ask if it is clean.
I will reply.
'It is clean! It is clean! It is clean!'
The woman will come in my house.

Beneath my house is the cellar
Where I keep the dirt I took out of the house.
If love is no use,
I will bring the dirt up out of the cellar;
I will put the dirt back in the house.
Women will walk by.

Lovely Dog

He was walking with you;
he walked over to me.
He's walking with me:
you've not got your lovely dog.

You look like a lonely man.
You look lonely because
you've not got your lovely dog.
I've got your lovely dog.

You look lost and lonely;
lost and lonely because
you've not got your lovely dog.
I've got your lovely dog.

We walk past your house.
You look out of your house.
You've not got your lovely dog:
I've got your lovely dog.

When he runs out of the river he
shakes off the water with a shiver that
starts with a flick of the tail and
ripples over the rows of his ribs
all the way to a quiver of his nose.

Lullaby

The birds are dropping down to their nests
for some supper and a rest.
Back home in their hives,
men-bees are buzzing 'Goodnight' to their wives.
In their drawers, spoons and forks
dream with the knives.

Darling, the sun's fallen off the edge
of our rented window ledge:
sleep, darling, please try.
You're all fat on my milk; your nappy's dry.
Shall I sway you in my arms,
or let you lie?

What should I do when you fret and twist?
Hey, don't frown. Don't bite your fist.
Please don't turn out bad.
You're a good looker, and so was your dad.
I wish I knew why he went.
Be a nice lad.

I thought my boyfriend and bump would be
my husband and family.
Wow, I was a chump.
He just picked a row, and then chose the hump:
before you were even born,
we'd both been dumped.

I just can't believe that the bastard
couldn't send his kid a card.
How couldn't he, how?
When I hunt down the bitch he's fucking now
I'm going to tear the cunt
out of the cow.

Happy birthday, my one and only.
I'm sorry I'm so moany.
It'll soon be your third,
and I'll have to leave off such pitiful words
and go back to singing
about the birds.

My darling, our lives won't have been wrecked
if I can make yours perfect.
I'd move off the sun
so you could sleep in the shade, little bun.
I'll do the suffering:
we'll have the fun.

The birds are dropping down to their nests
for some supper and a rest.
Back home in their hives,
Men-bees are buzzing 'Goodnight' to their wives.
In their drawers, spoons and forks
dream with the knives.

Misery

Come on in and shut the door.
I'm down here on the floor,
among the bills and circulars,
newspapers and letters.
It's nearly nice to see you again.
You look much the same.
Me? I know I look a mess –
just the way you like me best.

Come on through and find a seat.
There's no one here for you to meet.
Nothing here to eat or drink –
just the cooker, fridge and sink.
We'll watch the dishes fuzz,
listen to the black flies buzz.
We'll sit, and blink, and breathe,
waiting for the light to leave.

When we've sat in every chair,
carry me slowly up the stairs.
I've drawn the curtains to.
I've unmade the bed for you.
Hold me still, and gently coax
me out of making little jokes.
Lay me down before I fall.
Turn my face against the wall.

Monkey's in the Shed

I work hard
to make a sort of lard
from sweat and dirt
inside my shirt.
This rich grease
crawls in each new crease,
each old crack
of my neck and back.
By morning,
amazing spawning!
Monkey says,
'Sit down,'
wraps his legs around
my waist:
I brace.

Blackheads in their holes,
jumping out like tadpoles!

The light is brown;
black flies fly round.
Wet heat rots;
Monkey squats.
I take off my shirt:
Monkey goes to work,
puckers his lips,
grips me
so softly;
Monkey,
keen as mustard,
kind as custard,
unbuttons my back
and my fat is slack.

Monkey's in the shed!
Monkey does your blackheads!

Monkey's Not in the Shed

The last song was not true;
I have been singing lies to you.
You have been misled:
there was no monkey,
merely a shed.
This is what really happened.

My brother came to see me.
He said, 'You're so slow, boring:
I worry, my brother.
You're sullen, bored.
not the sporty sort of fellow
who taught me all I know
about fun and duty.
I'm worried, and so's Mother.
You're just not the same chap:
don't you ever leave the flat?
You really need new scenery.
We think some far off country.
Me and you! Sun, sand and sea
would stand us both fine and dandy.'
'No; I have important things to do.'

'It's beautiful, and cheap.'
'No; I have important things to do.'
'The fruit is so sweet.'
'No; I have important things to do.'
'The girls will make you weep.'
'No; I have important things to do.'
'We can lie on the beach and sleep.'
'No; I have important things to do.'
'Feel hot sand under our feet.'
'No; I have important things to do.'
'It'll be my treat.'
'No; I have important things to do.'
'You can bring your own Shredded Wheat.'
'No; I have important things to do.'

37

'We can hire a Jeep.'
'No; I have important things to do.'
'We can watch strange animals leap
across picturesque streets
in a haze of mellow heat
as we beep the horn of our Jeep.'
'No; I have important things to do.'
Then, sweetly, and brightly
My brother whispered to me.

'There's what?'
'A shed.'
'What, a shed?'
'Yes, a shed.'
'And a monkey?'
'Yes, a monkey.'
'A monkey monkey?'
'Yes, a monkey monkey.'
'A real monkey monkey?'
'Yes.'
'And the monkey's in the shed?'
'Yes.'
'And the monkey does your blackheads?'
'Yes'
'Right, there's a real monkey, in a shed,
that does your blackheads?'
'Yes.'

We ate the cheap sweet fruit
with the Shredded Wheat I brought.
We smiled at the girls
as we lay on the beach
among the inexpensive beauty,
in the shorts my brother bought.
We walked on hot sand,
and I got a nice tan,
and we watched strange animals leap
across picturesque streets
in a haze of mellow heat

as we beeped the horn of our Jeep.
Every day, it was a lot of fun.
Every day, I asked,
'Can I see the monkey now?'

'Monkey?'
'Yes, monkey.'
'What monkey?'
'The monkey monkey. The
monkey in the shed.'
'In the shed?'
'In the shed.'
'Shed?'
'Shed. Shed. Shed.'
'Monkey?'
'Yes, the monkey in the shed. That
does your blackheads. That
every day I ask to go and see, and
you always say, "some other day."
That monkey.'
'O, right. That monkey.'

'So that's the shed.'
'Yes.'
'The shed with the monkey in it.'
'Yes.'
'That does your blackheads?'
'Yes.'
'I'm so happy.'
'Right, I'll wait outside.'

'Aren't you coming in?'
'No. It's alright.'

'There's no monkey.'

'It must be out.'

Moon-sick

She was slack
in the bath.
With a ping
a pale fing-
ernail clip-

ping shot up,
and I marked
it's quick spark-
ling high arc
in the slip-

pery soft
candle light,
and the end
of it's flight
in the dark.

I looked o-
ver and smiled,
and she grinned
and contin-
ued her chore.

And now on
the unpicked-
up black knick-
ers she flicked
to the floor

that stray nail's
crescent rests.
When she'd dried,
she got dressed.
40   I'm moon-sick.

My Penis

I show my Penis my hand.
It does not seem to understand.
I place my Penis in my hand
and make a tender fist.
My Penis does not stand.
I work my wrist:
my Penis lists.
It is a useless Penis.

I show it romantic and filthy thoughts.
It stays short.
My scrotum is taut.
My scrotum is taut with too much sperm.
Too much sperm:
it burns, it burns.
My Penis is a disappointment.

I show my penis women.
It looks right through them.
The women are kind:
the women undress.
My Penis could not care less.
I apologise to the women;
'It is not you.
It is the Penis.
It is a useless Penis.'

I show my Penis a man.
I show it men,
I show it ten:
it will not stand.
It sits in my hand.
My Penis is a disappointment.

I take my Penis to school.
I show it children
– 'Good Morning, Penis.' –
I feel like a fool.
I show it boys.
I show it girls.
Nether boy nor girl
can coax my Penis to uncurl.
My Penis is a disappointment.

I take my Penis to the farm.
I show it a lamb.
I show it a bull.
Perhaps the leather?
Perhaps the wool?
My testicles stay full.
I take my Penis to the zoo.
I don't know what to do
about my Penis.
It is a useless Penis.

I beg my penis.
It hangs against my leg.
I shout at it:
'you are so negative!'
I blow it kisses.
I call it names.
I make my Penis promises.
I try to explain.
I do not rate my Penis.
All it does is urinate.

I show my penis a doctor.
Still it does not stir.
I show it a glove, cars, furniture;
I offer a beer;
I am forceful with spurs;
I show it a bishop, Birmingham, strawberry jam, cars, knitting,
every flower in the garden:
still it does not harden.
My Penis is a disappointment.

Is it bored?
A trip abroad?
I would take it to the moon!
I sing it tunes.
Does it wish it was warmer?
How about a sauna?
It will not get HARD!

My Penis just stares down.
My tears make a puddle on the ground.
In the puddle on the ground,
my Penis sees my Penis.

Ooh!

Names of Trees

I see the birds
stand in the trees:
I hear them sing
the names of trees.

I see the bugs
walk on the trees:
I hear them hum
the names of trees.

I would give the names of all the things I know to know the
names of trees

I see the pigs
take fruit from trees:
I hear them grunt
the names of trees.

'Tree, tree', I shout;
I shout, 'Tree, tree!'
I do not know
the names of trees.

I would give the names of all the things I know to know the
names of trees

The New Man

At last, I found somewhere far from roads
and flattish. I cleared up rocks, weed, rubbish and sowed.
I mowed the grass low, combed and tended.
When it was perfect, I blacked my boots and mended
my ball; played keepy-up, three and in;
imagining teams, I took turns to let each win.

One day, a man stopped and stood and looked.
When the ball dropped near to him, carefully he hooked
it back. Everyday, we stuck up sticks
and took turns to keep goal and take penalty kicks.
One day a new man stood, watched and waited.
When a wayward shot strayed near, he kicked it straight

back to my boot. We three practised skills —
how to trap the ball dead, dribble, pass, shoot, head, 'til
one fine day four men took turns to play
with and against each other, in two teams. Hooray!
Sometimes, the sun shone; sometimes, rain poured.
In time, more men came. Sun shone. Sometimes, rain poured.

We played keen and fair — no referee.
When a team won, there was no story, no trophy.
Then one great day, in that green field,
twenty-one men stood, shook each others' hands and kneeled,
did up their laces, pulled up their socks,
nodded, and kicked off, on that field among the rocks.

I heard breath sing our lungs raw, the blurred
thud of boots against ball and mud, and I heard birds.
At dark, knackered, jaw slack, loose on boneless
legs, each man walked back, I suppose, to his home.
Next day, the new man arrived, and asked
to play. Some poor fool passed him the ball, and the arse—

fart said, 'Thank you', and flicked it on straight
to a forward, who scored. New Man called, 'Great goal mate!
Hi! My name's Paul. What's yours?' I ignored
the bore. A good footballer? He could not shut up for
a whole minute. Worse, the other chaps
started to encourage, comment, and all-round yap.

I mowed the grass low, combed and tended.
When it was perfectly flat from green end to end,
I blacked my boots, and as I'd rended
the last ball in pieces, painstakingly I mended
it. I kneeled, and less twenty one, did
up my laces, pulled up my socks, attacked and defended.

Oblong

Rectangles argue with the trees;
Oblongs lie at length with ease.
Rectangles have no memory;
Oblongs know your family.

I see my friend;
I feel oblong.
The day is kind;
I feel oblong.

I meet some wood;
I feel oblong.
I eat some cake;
I feel oblong.

We score a goal;
I shout 'Oblong'.
We lose a goal;
'O, rectangle!'

I will not say 'rectangle'
When I can say 'oblong'.
'Rectangle' and 'rectangular':
Both of them are wrong.

Oliver

My friend Oliver
was a fine scholar
with a clean collar.
Ollie was an athlete;
Mr Lee was an aesthete.
That's why he put Ollie's feet
on either side of his ears,
and Ollie asked me, 'Does that mean I'm queer?'

Ollie got star parts,
was good at art
and top of his class.
He was a fast bowler,
and he scored the last goal.
He never knew he had an arsehole
until the blighter showed him
it was pink with a puckery rim.

I looked rotten,
like an old blotter.
I'd lots of spots
from rubbing marge on my face
and in other places.
I'd have burst in Mr Lees' embrace.
You know I even thought
if I rubbed myself with a toad I'd get warts.

My school report
said 'bad at sports,
attention span short,
poor attitude and aptitude,
sullen to the point of rude,
caught with a toad in the nude.'
They never guessed how much work
it took to be such an unattractive berk.

I thought I'd better tell
Ollie how to smell.
I searched for well
over an hour until I found
him up on the hill looking at the town.
I sat my dirty arse down
next to Ollie on the top step.
I said, 'Ollie, best be inept.'

On the Meadows

One slow drop, another,
now two drops together –
one breaks upon my nose's tip,
one softly on this lip.

And from the moon's far side
out slips half a smile,
a peeping eye seeks mine.
I kiss a cheek, it shines.

She reaches to unsettle
one wet daisy petal
from my christened brow and shows
me how it's on her fingertip now.

One of Two

One armpit is as naked as the hollow
of a sea-washed shell.

One armpit is as hairy as the woods
where all the wild beasts dwell.

Plank

By the sea, I found a plank.
By the sea, I found a plank.
I found a plank by the sea.

Over the hill, I took my plank.
Over the hill, I took my plank.
I took my plank over the hill.

In the night, the sea came over the hill.
In the night, the sea came over the hill.
The sea came over the hill in the night.

I'm learning to sleep on a plank in the sea.

A Row of Poplars

Like feathers stuck in the ground
the Poplars sway a little,
trying to give the clouds'
low heavy bellies a tickle.

Sailor Song

My memory admires the young recruits
in bright white uniforms and burnished boots
who trotted up the old gang-plank
to stand on deck in nervous rank.
Curling my remarkable moustaches,
I exercised my long eye-lashes.

> *When I die – and the day is soon –*
> *have my body hauled from this room.*
> *Give a job to a boy in a boat:*
> *to float far out to sea, and there to lob*
> *me, and my precious hoard, overboard to bob.*

On the bridge, I smiled; so glad and sure
a queue would form outside my door.
Extending, then, a cordial hand,
I'd gently pull the foremost man
into my congenial little cabin,
and chuck him underneath the chin.

After the pleasure of our exertion, and
some inconsequential conversation
concerning life in the big tin tub,
I'd don my apron and cook up grub.
My chum would yawn and, in my arms,
dream of my cooking, cock and charms.

But I could hardly sleep a single wink,
in anticipation of the merry stink,
which, at the very crack of dawn,
would make my tiny cabin warm:
a brown length in an enamel dish
would satisfy my dearest wish.

For, at first light, lifting up his shirt
I watched each lad's sweet arse-dirt
stretch, and softly drop into my dish,
pert in its mist, to perfectly astonish.
Those lads fought harder to love me
than they did for any Majesty.

Save for one little lad who had the squits,
each lad I slept with left me a shit –
one turd so long I kept it in halves.
Old sailors choose diaries, letters, photographs
to usher them back through the years
to dim islands where they spend their tears.

And some carve little ships. With shaky hands
they sail them in bottles on little stands.
I procured a supply of such stands myself,
to effect the display of my great wealth:
each turd, once eased from out the dish,
was slowly sealed with strokes of varnish.

These rolling decks and I massaged the straight
from many a grateful winger's gait.
Ship's positions, names and dates
inscribed beneath on golden plates,
my deep and darkening gifts of excrement
save me from disappointment in the present.

Scarborough

So here's all of Scarborough:
the castle and its towers,
the church and its high spire,
all the shops and houses,
and the boats in the harbour.
The wind blows for miles –
it's a little hard on hairstyles.
You'll laugh if you don't smile.

On some late afternoons
in winter, there's a moon
in a sky of greys as luminous
as Mum's mother-of-pearl is.
It'll be that time soon.
We could just pause here,
among the scent of lavender,
and see if it appears.

Scoff it Up

Forget that stupid vet.
You mustn't die yet.
I'm not ready, so:
on your marks, set, go –

> *Scoff it up –*
> *you coughed it up.*
> *Lick it up*
> *you dirty dog.*

What if I pick out the best bits?
Or put sugar on it?
What if I fried it up?
C'mon, fried with ketchup?

You're too thin.
Get your soggy chin
up off the deck,
get that lot back down your neck.

That's the last tin,
and all of my din-dins,
so stop mucking about
and move that fucking snout.

Be a good hound
or I'll have you put down
and buy a cute little pup
that drinks milk from a teacup.

You think because you're old
you don't have to do what you're told.
Wrong. Stop hacking
and get that lot back in.

Look, I'm down on my knees.
C'mon, pretty please.
Begging's supposed to be your job.
Open your fucking gob.

Don't sick up your pills.
You never used to be ill.
Eat up while I get my hat.
We'll go out and chase cats!

Shopping Trolley

I pushed my shopping trolley
to a broken house,
and there I found,
among the rubbish,
some things to keep or sell:
a coat with a fur collar;
a saucepan with no holes,
and a small child's shoe.

When I was ten
I was to be, at twenty-six,
a Captain or a Major.
But here I am
in a light rain
with a new coat,
pushing my shopping home.

When I was ten
the Colonel caught me
as I kissed his daughter.
But he said this did not matter:
he held my shoulder,
made me promise
to be, one day, his Major.

The coat with the fur collar
I shall probably keep,
the saucepan, sell –
oh, and some nails.
I would kiss again his daughter,
but I would not be his Major.

Small Arsed Boy

I'd eaten dinner,
done the dishes –
keeping my hands warm
in the washing-up water –
knock on the door.
Huh?
It was a small arsed boy.
It was a small arsed boy
in a longish vest.
He had nothing on
but that vest –
some shoes.
He said,
'Lift up your dress,
and show me your shopping.'

So This is Why

So this is why I've come to a stop.
Oh what an eyeful, what a skyful!
Red below yellow, white on top –
is it a sunset or a trifle?

Sorry Dog

I would not get out of bed:
put my bottom out,
did it on the floor.
Dad hit the dog:
'You're a dirty, dirty –
you're a dirty dog.'

The dog looked long at me
where I lay in bed.
Hitting done,
Dad rubbed dog's face in it:
'You're a dirty, dirty –
you're a dirty dog.'

Each night, I did loads of it:
dog looked up at me.
Dad sent dog off
to be made dead.
I'm an ugly, ugly –
I'm an ugly man.

Dog, I'm sorry.
Sorry, dog.
I'm sorry, dog.
I've got biscuits,
toothbrush,
carpets –
I've got carpets for you, dog.
Come into my house, dog,
do it where you want, dog.
Do it on my leg, or,
if you like,
bite me so I bleed:
I'm an ugly man.
You're not a dirty dog.

Squarehead

We had no boy to hate:
We were all good mates;
none fat, or dumb, or lame.
Then the hats came.
Our hats came each in a round box.
His hat came – yes! – in a square box:
he was a Squarehead.
He asked, 'please check.'
We put our boxes on our heads.
We put his box – yes! – on his head.
Why beat Squarehead?
Because his head is square.
'Swear that your head is square, Squarehead.'
'Yes, my head is square.'

As a table, he was able.
For filling squarish gaps,
he was the perfect chap.
We hurt him hard,
but not as hard as when he said,
'I am not Squarehead.'
'Put your head in the box, boy!'

We stripped him nude,
stood on his cubes.
'Put your head in the box, boy!
Put your head in the box!'

We took his hair:
he got more square.
'Put your head in the box, boy!
Put your head in the box!'

We said, 'we find
that your smart lines
are spoilt by ears.'
We showed him shears.
Why beat Squarehead?
Because his head is square.
'Swear that your head is square, Squarehead.'
'Yes, my head is square.'

One day Squarehead said,
'I will not be Squarehead.'
'Put your head in the box, boy!
Put your head in the box!'

'Please change my name.'
We tried more pain.
'Put your head in the box, boy!
Put your head in the box!'

Still he said,
'I am not Squarehead.'
We said, 'Sad, untrue,
but we will help you.
We will tie you to this chair:
we will round your square.'

We had broken the stick:
We were using a brick.
Not round, but red,
Squarehead said,
'I am wrong.
Put my box on.
Please let me rest.'
We gave a test:
'Are these all equilateral rectangles?
Six sides, each as wide as tall,

should not be found upon a ball.'
Squarehead said,
'I am, and always will be, Squarehead.'
We put plasters where he bled.
He took the pillows from his bed.
On his books, he wrote, 'S. Head.'

Why beat Squarehead?
Because his head is square.
'Swear that your head is square, Squarehead?'
'Yes my head is square.'

One day, a new boy came,
not fat, or dumb, or lame.
His head was square.
We watched old Squarehead stare.
Happy, he said,
'My name is Ned.
Please have my box:
a blow to the block
hurts less in a box.
A blow to the block,
from brick, stick or rock,
hurts less in a box.
Please have my chair.'

Square Pears, Rare Bears

Square Pear Pair dare lair where Rare Bear Pair stare.

Square Pears flare their nares there.

Pears scare Bears.

Pears snare Bears.

Bears care. Bears share prayers.

Square Pear Pair tear Rare Bears fair hair.

Fair Square Pear Pair share Rare Bears fair hair.

Hair-spare Bears glare.

Hair-spare Bears swear.

Sweet and Tender Kisses

I thought all your sweet and tender kisses
were promises.
I thought I had a girlfriend:
I just had someone else's.

Which felt like stepping on a stair
that wasn't there,
and toppling headlong through
a mystery of air.

Now once again it seems to me
a memory
is at its best a sweet regret,
at worst, an enemy.

And the dark depths of your eyes were shadows
on shallows,
and the tree in which you carved our names
in a heart
was hollow.

Teaching a Lion to Roar

She's teaching a lion to roar:
'Come on, now, Leo, relax your jaw.
Open big and wide:
get everything in outside.
Next week we'll do
Lesson Two:
Knowing When To.'

'You just hang upside down in a heap.'
She's teaching a three-toed sloth how to sleep.
'Right, you hold on with this toe;
this toe's for not letting go,
and this one does both.
Let's not loaf
in the undergrowth!'

She's teaching a camel to drink.
She's led it to water; she's making it think.
'Look at that beast down there;
it's about to take your share.
From lip to rump
you're one big pump,
so fill your hump.'

They're both up a tree – she used cake.
The sloth is hanging, but it's wide awake.
She's drawn it some sheep and a gate.
'Now close your eyes, little mate,
and count all of those
leaping this as you doze –
only not on your toes.'

She's filled her bath up to the brim.
She's going to teach a fish how to swim.
There's a small singing bird in her hair.
Soon it'll conquer the air.
That shy skunk'll stink,
and the squid in the sink
start squirting ink.

Three Sweepers

Three sweepers sweep.
At dawn they sweep
the car park.
At dusk they sweep
again 'til dark.
Three sweepers sweep
and, soft, I weep
to hear them
softly sweep.
Three sweepers sweep
the car park clear.
They disappear.

All night our dust falls softly down.

Three sweepers sweep
softly, twice
a day I weep
on egg fried rice
I do not eat.
Three sweepers sweep.
They sweep slowly by
my restaurant seat.
Their brushes sigh.
They float in heat
and dust and tears.
Sweep near, sweep near.

All night our dust falls softly down.

Three sweepers sweep,
so sure, so slow,
as if in sleep.
Three sweepers sweep
the dust into a row
of seven heaps;
sweep their shadows
black and go.
I pause all day:
the dust will stray.

Toe

On the path I roll,
and unroll, and hold
my blue big toe. Don't laugh: it's not fun –
ny. I'd give some
of my money, if
I could only give
all of this hurt, pain and agony
to your body.

I wish it was you
who, without one shoe,
had thickened a toe against that brick,
and now felt sick.
Please cut off my leg –
or should I just beg
angels to descend with pills and fans
and waxen hands?

Faith, hope, charity:
They're nothing to me.
I roll and blow. O, both front and back,
my toe is black:
hurt, pain, agony
are thrice as nasty
as happiness, joy and ecstasy
are nice to me.

You see how hurt, pain
and agony lame
my toe? Without leaving their first home,
the bastards roam –
ankle, groin, gut, neck –
grab, rejoice and wreck:
I sob. Up into my head, the louts
lob bombs about.

They burst in my head:
red, black, red, black, red,
red. I'd stamp the whole wrong world to dirt
to stop this hurt,
pain and agony
happening to me.
People could die, I know. I'm sorry,
but they're not me.

Slack seconds sour.
Minutes mock hours.
Blackness binds me, broken, to the path.
The bastards laugh,
and stroll, whistling, down
to my guts, and round
for a bit, and jump about and slump
in a lump, plump

with bad fun. They sigh,
itch, yawn. Sleep, boys. My
battered brain is furred with many blurred
and loathsome words.
I grovel, prostrate,
in cowardly hate
of everything, grind my frown down
into the ground.

I struggle, supine,
to filthy sunshine.
Tears trickle into my ears. They dry.
I look at sky.
Far away, my toe
shrinks back to its row.
I summon strength, crawl under a shrub
and softly rub.

Tree Bees in a Bee Tree

Mummy said to me,
'Let's wake up Daddy
to take us to see
the Bee Tree.'

We three went to see
a lovely Bee Tree.
It was summery
with Tree Bees.

Bee Trees like Tree Bees
being in their leaves.
Tree Bees like to be
in Bee Trees.

My Mummy and me
stood back from Daddy.
He said, 'Look laddy,
see: bees, trees.'

Daddy said, 'Let me
tell you both of bees.
They live high in trees.
They're stripy.

They're stripy, furry,
and sound all whirry,
because of their wings.'
O Daddy.

'Daddy, O Daddy,
these bees sting, Daddy.
They sting, believe me.
They're tree bees.'

Me and my Mummy
saw the Bee Tree freeze.
We saw the Bee Tree
sneeze the bees.

We saw the Bee Tree
empty of Tree Bees.
We watched my silly
Daddy flee.

Turning German

I want to have fun in a tree.
I cannot have fun in a tree
when I am not a monkey.
When I am not a monkey
it makes me as sad as an empty tree.
When I am as sad as an empty tree
it makes me angry.
It makes me angry as a German man
who cannot have fun in a tree. God
damn! God damn! Got un dam!
Oh no. Acht zo! Ya ya:
Nicht no. Nein nein. Ya ya:

I think I'm turning German.
I want to be a monkey.

Ich merchte zu climben ein grossen pine.
Ich immer gefallen zu der ground
mit ein Deutsche sound.
Alles ist scheisse. Ja, ist sehr scheisse.
Ich nicht gelike eidelweiss.